A Forgiving Heart Moves Forward

Shelia Mansfield

MISSION POSSIBLE PRESS
Creating Legacies through Absolute Good Works

The Mission is Possible.

Sharing love and wisdom for the young and "the young at heart," expanding minds, restoring kindness through good thoughts, feelings, and attitudes is our intent. May you thrive and be good in all you are and all you do…

Be Cause U.R. Absolute Good!

A Forgiving Heart Moves Forward

© 2018 by Shelia Mansfield

No part of this book may be reproduced in any written, electronic, recording, or photocopying form without written permission of the publisher. The exception would be in the case of brief quotations embodied in critical articles or reviews and pages where permission is specifically granted by the publisher.

Although every precaution has been taken to verify the accuracy of the information contained herein, the author and publisher assume no responsibility for any errors or omissions. No liability is assumed for damages that may result from the use of information contained within. All rights reserved worldwide.

Books may be purchased in quantity by contacting the publisher directly:

Mission Possible Press, A division of Absolute Good,

PO Box 8039 St. Louis, MO 63156

or by calling 240.644.2500

MissionPossiblePress.com

ISBN: 978-0-9996766-1-5

First Edition Printed in the United States

Acknowledgements

Special thanks to my children Shreela, Titus (Valerie) and Tenell (Christie), for always loving and encouraging me.

I'd like to thank my niece, Maya, who sat down and typed all of my handwritten poems for this book. I'm from the horse and buggy days and I couldn't have done it without her!

Thank you to my sister, Ina, for having my back during my times of struggle and for making me see that I can do anything even when I didn't feel courageous.

Thanks to Leola, my mother's friend, for mothering me through these years of struggle and victory. Thanks to my friends, Florence in California, Bobbie in Texas, and Brenda in Illinois, Dr. Dorothy for pushing me to take that writing class, and all of my friends in St. Louis who have encouraged me to write.

Thank you to my publisher, Jo Lena Johnson who believed in me when other publishers didn't. She made me feel like I was a person and not a joke. The way she treated me made me feel renewed. Expressing myself allowed me to free up some of that old storage that had been locked up for years.

Contents

Hey There! 1
In the Beginning 3
Opening the Door 5
They Must Pay 8
Life Choices 9
The Second I Do 14
The Struggle 21

Poems
Take Your Time 22
Girlfriend, Evict or Acquit 23
Human Error 26
Alone 27
The Husband 28
Hell Raiser 30
A Slave Was Made 31
A Slave and Maid Has a Prayer 32
He Seeks the Weak 34
I am a Victor 35
Anxiety 37
Without 38
What's in it for Me? 39
What's Wrong with You? 40
Do You Mean It? 42
Mind 43
Hello, Holler, Holla 44

Dear Dr. Jiggly Wiggly 45
I Eat 46
Smaller Caboose 47
Really? 48
The Eraser 49
Secrets Don't Serve 50
Power of the Tongue 52
Eyes 53
Amazing 54
Evidently 55
Appreciation 56
Rainbows 58
Know No 59
Laughing 60
The Key 61
Getting to the New Me 62
Moving Along 64
Divorce 65
#MeToo 66
Grudges 67
A Recipe for Grace 68
Birth of a Child 69

Why Did I Stay? 71
Reality Check 75
About the Author 78

Hey There!

I love writing poetry in rhyming style,
telling stories about true life.
Including things I think and experience,
life, too full of strife.
Things you think but might be too scared to
talk about.
I want to make you think.
To help you do something about your circumstance.

A Forgiving Heart Moves Forward
is about life situations and it's real.
I'm finally opening my mouth to spill the deal.
I lived, nearly died. Existing in a house full of lies.
It wasn't right and wasn't fair, yet I chose for too many
years to stay there.

Don't be like me, I want you to see…
See with eyes opened wide and not shut.
Don't allow anyone to kick your butt.

Patience has been counting down to blast off.
Cough. Cough. Cough.

What is in your way? Do you dare say?
Get a fresh start and learn to laugh and not die.
Fill your heart with love and let that multiply.
Breathe and let go.
Live to have inner peace flow.
~ Shelia

In the Beginning

"I was loved very much by my parents and grandmother."

I was born February 7, 1945, the youngest of four children. My parents were married. My father had his own business as a window washer for the shops in downtown St. Louis on Locust Street. He employed three other people, besides himself. He was making $200 a week, back then, which was a lot of money. My mother sold real estate, as a part-time career. We were the first blacks to move into the Central West End area of the city, an upscale neighborhood. We always ate at the dinner table as a family, with meals prepared by my mother. We had to say our blessing. We were not allowed to drink anything until we finished our food. If we didn't like the food, we would sneak it under the table and give it to our dog, Snookie. We cleaned up after we ate the meals, as we didn't have distractions like the telephone or television.

After dinner, my father would help us study. My sister would be our entertainment by playing the piano as I waltzed with my father, my little feet on top of his as we danced. As we did that, my brother was taking apart toys and putting them back together. He was always good at that.

We had big Christmas celebrations as my dad fixed up the house and the yard, even winning neighborhood awards for his efforts. Though my memory is a little cloudy about that time long ago, I do remember one Christmas when I was about five years old. One of my father's old friends came over bearing gifts. Mine was a box full of little girl panties which had the days of the week imprinted on each pair. My daddy cussed him out, told him to take them back and dare not give his daughter panties or anything else like that again. I don't remember seeing him come back over.

"Daddy stood up for me."

Opening the Door

"One day changed my view of myself and of life."

When I was five years old my parents had to leave to go and show a house. They told me not to open the door for anybody.

A little while after they left, the neighbor, two doors down, came a knocking.

He told me that my daddy sent him to get a tool and to let him in. I saw a tool on the table and thought it would be okay to open the door.

I remember taking the chain off of the door and letting him in the house. I remember sitting on his lap, facing him, his crusty old wrinkled man-part and the odor of him as he rubbed his thing close to mine. How did he get my panties off? I don't know. He tried to put that in me. On the green striped and crème loveseat, trimmed with wood, standing on claw-feet.

I told my mother what happened and I don't remember what happened after that. It's as if I blocked it out.

After my parents' divorce, when I was 12, we moved and my dad stayed at that house. Sometimes when I was there, that man visited my dad in the garage, tinkering with tools. Yet, he never came close to me again until one day when I was 13 and coming back from the confectionary, crossing the street.

He came from out of nowhere, putting his big black hand on my forearm as if he had the right. He asked, "What did I ever do to you?" I had never cussed before but I called him every name I had ever heard and ran across the street, right into my daddy's house.

What Happened?

Later, as an adult, I was speaking to my mother's first cousin, talking about that man. I was surprised she knew about what happened. She told me that my mother didn't tell my daddy because my daddy was hot tempered and she knew he would kill that man.

I wished for many years he would have killed him. I never really felt safe after that and believe that affected my confidence and my self-esteem. It's not until now that I can think, with confidence that my mother probably took matters into her own hands, which is why he made that statement. However, it doesn't help me with the way I saw myself and felt inferior for most of my life.

"Unfortunately, Daddy was unable to protect me."

I didn't want to say.
I don't want anyone to be mad at me and I don't want to hurt anybody.

I just didn't know why that nobody hurt my body.
…And my mind, and my soul, and my life.

They Must Pay

*If you know someone has abused a child,
you must make them pay.*

It may not be that day, but find some way.

*I'm not saying kill them, but don't shield them.
There is another way.*

*Opening the door to healing is where you must stay and
that takes making those terrible suckers pay!*

Life Choices

*"I made bad choices and married early,
when I was 17 years old."*

My father took care of home. We had nice things, and he took care of us. After my parents divorced he continued to support us. However, my mother was independent and knew that ultimately she had to take care of us. As I was growing up, "they" say my father fought/abused my mother, but I never saw that. Momma told me that the day the divorce was final she walked across the street from the courthouse and put in an application at Union Electric. When she got home, the phone was ringing. They offered her a job, and she took it. Momma worked there until she retired, at least 30 years. She sent my sister to college. My brother joined the Marines.

Married at 17

I made bad choices and married early, when I was 17 years old. We lived together in the Peabody Darst Webbe projects in St. Louis, with our three children. My husband was an alcoholic. It was an abusive marriage. One night when we were fighting, he hit me so hard that one of our sons fell out of my arms onto the concrete floor. He was injured, but I thank God there was no permanent damage to him.

Though he was working, only occasionally would he give me money for food. One day when my mother came to visit and saw there was only beer and whiskey in the refrigerator, she started buying groceries so the kids and I could eat. We continued to fight. The only job I had was part-time babysitting for our neighbor, who also lived in the projects. She didn't have any money, because she just started the job, so I didn't charge her to watch the two kids.

One day I went to the breezeway and saw my husband get out of the car with groceries in hand, and go to her apartment, not ours. When she opened the door for him, they embraced and kissed. I put on his old black trench coat with hospital socks, slipping on the closest things I could. I walked over to that apartment and banged on the door. When she opened the door she said, "He made me do it…" She and I had a few choice words but he didn't come to the door. When he made it back to our apartment we got into another fight.

The next morning she came over and brought her kids as if I was still going to babysit them. It was hard for me to say no, but I couldn't and wouldn't do it. I don't know what happened with her and that job or if they continued to see each other but I stayed with him. I wanted to get out of the marriage but I didn't have any income.

California

Fortunately, his friend told him about a job opportunity with Douglas Aircraft in California. He went out there, got the job and lived with the friend and his wife. When he left for California, I was glad that he went. Since he just started the job we did not have enough money for the kids and I to keep the apartment. After we moved in with my mother, I felt like we were being a burden on her. So, when he called for us to join him, I didn't want to go but felt it was best. My mother insisted that my daughter stay with her and my sister, promising to give her the best education, dancing lessons and other skills. It was hard for me to leave without her but knowing how horrible he was, I felt it was best for her.

Eventually, he sent for me and the boys. We took the train to Los Angeles, moving into a 33 unit apartment building he was managing there. This was in addition to his full-time job. He was an alcoholic and got fired from the full-time job for having alcohol on the premise and for drinking. Less than six months after the boys and I got to L.A., he got a call that there was a family crisis in St. Louis. He decided to go and see about it, taking the rent he had collected from all of the tenants to pay for his trip. When the building owner came looking for him, I told him the truth. He was angry and said he would press charges. He also told me I should have never married that man. The building's owner gave me a month to live there and to find a new place to live, though he turned off the utilities in our apartment.

I had no skills, no driver's license and couldn't qualify for welfare because I hadn't lived in the state long enough. I had begun collecting bottles and cans for the deposit money, even going into the dumpsters at times, to get them. Someone told me to go to the Urban League for help. I went there and was honest about my situation. The man made a call to Douglas Aircraft and told me how to take the bus to get there. I lived in an area called, "The Jungle" located in South Central L.A., which took almost two hours on the bus to get to Long Beach, where Douglas was located. When they told me I was hired I was in shock and admitted that I didn't have clothes to wear to work or bus fare to get there. They advanced me a week's salary and let me go into the company store to get clothes to wear.

My first job was delivering mail on a three-wheeled scooter on the campus that I had to learn how to drive. I got a few promotions along the way even though I was late every day for the first six months, trying to get the kids and myself situated.

My husband never came back to us. I never spoke to him after he left. I filed for divorce by using the court and notices in the newspaper. He never answered the paperwork. I had endured him for eight years and it was finally over. I was told he was put in prison for his crime of theft. Years later, the kids did connect with their dad, but I was not part of that.

Back to St. Louis

We continued to live in California for several more years until my mother became ill. I quit my job and we moved back to St. Louis to care for momma. I got a job at a local manufacturing company, working in the factory and in the laboratories; that was 1972.

"I was an abandoned young mother with kids to feed, working in a factory."

The Second I Do

"He's like a chameleon, however the man was a narcissistic, flirtatious and mean spirited abuser."

Despite what my husband took me through, my outside appearance was kept up. I was cute and was shapely, built up, with blonde hair. That same year I met my second husband at a bowling alley. He was with a man I knew. Our mutual friend saw me; he came over and introduced me to him. The first thing he said to me was, "May I have your autograph?" I thought that was weird but I let it go. Talking to him, it was just something to do. When he asked me for my telephone number, I gave him the number and he gave me his. I wasn't really attracted to him, but I went along with it.

We continued the conversation. In one breathe he said he wasn't married then in the next breathe he said he was getting a divorce, and living separately. So, he lied immediately.

We went our separate ways. Later, I told my girlfriend I met this dude. She was single too so she told me to call him up so we could get together, as long as he could bring a friend. The only reason I called him that Sunday morning was because of her. He and I discussed a visit. He and his friend picked me up so we could go to her house, play cards and have a few drinks. When she opened the door and let the friend in first, he went in second. She whispered to me, "This one is mine," pointing to mine. I said, "No that one is mine." I wished I had never said that because I really wasn't attracted to him but since she was really wanting him that's what made me change my mind. Isn't that a shame? That was my biggest mistake.

A Good Man?

My mother always said if you meet a good man keep him. To her, a good man meant a man with a good job. Back then, after we started dating, he was giving me $100 a week. Money meant a lot to me because I didn't have any. Yet, he was really strict. He acted like a father, telling me what I wasn't supposed to do and he had rules and regulations about everything. I was only allowed to show affection at his discretion. He expected more of me than of himself. The signs were there but I didn't pay attention to them as we were dating.

He owned two houses when we met and I was living in an apartment. When his divorce was final, he gave the ex-wife one of the houses. When my lease was up, we moved into the other house with him. Once I moved in, he would say cruel things to me. I would wait on him hand and foot.

One time we got into it so bad that he told me to get out of "his house." I didn't leave right then but called my mother to get the savings bonds I had given her to keep from my days working in California. I used the money to purchase my own house. As soon as it was done, the kids and I moved into that house. Instead of leaving well-enough alone, I made the mistake of showing off my house to him. That opened the door for him to say he could make improvements and such on my house. That led to us fixing the house up and him trying to come back in. I let him back in. We got married about a year after we met.

He and his youngest daughter, who was a senior in high school, moved into my house. He craved the spotlight and wanted to be the center of attention. Almost immediately he started calling me and my boys' names. He would say things which were very demeaning, especially under his breathe. I responded by cussing him out. I began hating him. I started gaining weight.

My kids didn't like him even at the ages of 9, 10 and 11. When we would argue, he would say, "I'll get my hat and coat and leave." The kids would get his hat and coat, holding them at the door, waiting for him to leave. He would never leave. He would tell me I would never make it without him. When the kids would complain to me, I would tell them, "You aren't going to make me lose my man," just like my momma used to tell me when she was married to my stepfather.

I kept waiting on him, doing things for him, even leaving my job to go home daily to fix his meals and go back to work. We didn't get along. If I didn't want to do something he would say, "This is your womanly duty. If I didn't do what I was supposed to do as the man, you wouldn't like it so do what you are supposed to do."

The Mistreatment Became Unbearable

In the late 80's between the abuse at home and seeing the prejudice on my factory job, the discrimination became too severe for me to handle. The way we were treated as Black people and the way I was talked to caused me to cry every time I would drive on the street where my job was, which meant I cried almost as soon as I got in the car, since the factory was five minutes from our home.

I would go home on my break about 4 a.m. no matter if it was snow or ice to fix food for my family. I felt obligated to go home and fix breakfast and lunch for him to take to work. One day I packed a big old Vidalia onion and chips as his lunch, by themselves. It was payback for the way he continued to treat me, and I felt good about doing it. Of course he was upset but I wasn't. I was a total mess, mentally. After many years of marriage, I just couldn't take any more so I couldn't stop crying on the job. The nurse said for me to call my doctor. She knew some of the things I was going through. She said, "Shelia you can go down so low that you can't get up." I left the job and called my doctor. I had to be treated for severe depression.

I was afraid to be admitted in the hospital but I couldn't stop crying. Also I thought it would be like the movie, *"One*

Flew Over the Cuckoo's Nest." But it wasn't. I was on the floor with people who suffered from major depression like me. After several weeks of calling him, I started catching the bus to go home and fix dinner. I would get back in time for meds. It was like a vacation for me because I didn't have to be criticized, felt relaxed and didn't have to deal with him flirting with other women and drinking. It was better than any trip I ever took with him to Europe, Africa or the Islands.

When I was released from the hospital, I was back into the same environment. I began the same routine, waiting on him hand and foot. I endured the joaning. He wasn't going to change and for some reason, I couldn't change. The telltale signs were there but I just didn't listen, nor learn.

Going back didn't make it any better, but my God was there with me. I was pressed between he and Thee.

Never let yourself get controlled and in a rut by he but be controlled by the One and only Omniscient, Omnipotent Father. He will carry us through each and every day. Just remember to put Him first and keep Him there.

I Didn't Listen

Between 2002 and 2006 I had five calcified cysts in the same area. I was hospitalized for over a month in Minnesota as a result. When I was discharged, I would ask him to massage the area to help with my healing. Instead of helping, he would take his hand and rub hard, just to hurt me, so I would tell him to stop and I would stop asking. He was a controlling, narcissistic, polished alcoholic who knew how to charm. I did what I was supposed to do for 42 years.

My health continued to deteriorate during the marriage. When he had knee replacements, I continued to serve him. I'll never forget the day I heard my nine-year-old great grandchild say, "Pa-pa treats Gambie like a slave." When I heard that it bothered me enough to realize I was being stupid, and that everyone else, including a small child could see what I would not see. To date, I've had over 10 operations, some of them as a result of the abuse I endured.

I used to lie to everyone, including my children, about what was happening in our home. As adults, I didn't want my children to hurt him, which I knew they would have, had they known the truth. I lied to the doctors about the abuse when I went to the hospital. I couldn't lie anymore, the last time my wrist was broken, the second time in the same year. I was so miserable and so numb, I no longer felt pain. With the doctor's support and encouragement, I decided I didn't want to die. That was going to be the last time. Not just because I found the courage, but because I had support, since I had been keeping the bruises and scars a secret.

I decided to get divorced. I filed for divorce. We got divorced.

So many times I've felt like a fool for staying with him, not believing I could make it on my own. But I didn't want to die.

Nobody should stay in an abusive situation. Nobody.

There is so much which hasn't been told, but I left it alone. I know you aren't supposed to hate, but I hated his guts. I prayed to God to take that hate away from me. The hate is gone but the memory is not.

Nobody should stay in an abusive situation. Nobody.

In my pain and in my healing, I wrote these poems. I've written this book because I wanted to feel like I accomplished something in my life. I hope that young or old will look at the total picture, and if you are in a similar situation, I hope you will turn around and leave. Evacuate the situation because they won't ever change.

"Do the scoping, not the choking so you can survive and stay alive, and report their hide."

The Struggle

"On those days when I feel off-track, I acknowledge the struggle, but I keep moving forward."

Sometimes I forget what is behind and struggle for what is ahead simultaneously. This is a daily challenge for me as I am trying to meet and reach my goals. Being positive, loving myself and forgiving others helps me to move forward, so that's what I concentrate on, especially when I find myself sinking or getting off track.

"Don't do what I did, do what I say, so you can wake up to see another day."

Take Your Time

What happens when a man or woman walks into your life out of nowhere?

Do you jump head over heels or do you take a moment to think?

Are you confusing emotion with action?

Should you procrastinate and take some time to pick a mate?

*In any moment of decision,
the best thing you can do is take your time to do the right thing.*

The next best thing is acting quickly and doing the wrong thing.

The worst thing you can do is nothing.

You do have choices and besides, what is the rush?

Girlfriend, Evict or Acquit

For all you ladies out there that are blindly in love and don't want to see.
Here is a little insight to help you decipher, hopefully.

When a man comes into your life
the warning signs are there, you must pay attention to the when and the where.

All men are not living in sloth, just know what you're cooking with in that broth.

When you have your blinders on, a void needs to be filled, however that doesn't justify going in undistilled.

Girlfriend, know when you need to acquit or evict…

You put your best foot forward and show him a good time, in essence, giving him a free ride.

While he's thinking,
"I'm in there, she's lucky she's mine."

Girlfriend, big mistake.

Before you know it, he's on the take.

He's moved in twenty four hours a day, five days a week.
Forget the weekends, he's gone and you are all alone and can't sleep.
Why be so sad, yet surprised when the whole picture was there before your eyes?
Yes, you failed to realize, listening to all his BS and jive.

You ask yourself...

"What was his agenda?"
"Why did he say he loves and needs me?"
"Where was his integrity?"
"What made me feel like we could be as one?"

Then you begin to feel undone...

Good Questions Girl...

Why didn't he look at your inner beauty instead of your sister-girl booty?

Treating you as another conquest?
It was all a test.

He was playing the mind game.

Girlfriend, get over the blame.

You feel dissected with this superficial love but a man who really loves you will treat you with kid-gloves.

Girlfriend, get over it.

*It's best to evict rather than acquit.
Look before you leap and avoid the grief.*

Human Error

He baits.
He hates.
He steals your thoughts.
He gives you joy.
He has you saying, "Boy, oh boy!"

You are now molded.
You are his pawn.
He is your joy.
He has you singing, "Boy, oh boy!"

He takes your pride.
He hates your self-esteem.
He steals your confidence.
You are his toy.
He has you shouting, "Boy, oh boy!"

Baiting, hating.

You once thought before the baiting.
You were a human being, but now, you're
the being controlled by the human.

Alone

I feel alone although you are near.

You can't help me 'cause you can't see or feel my inner thoughts of loneliness because you are not here.

I need some excitement to make me aware, cause being close doesn't put you there.

The Husband

The man I married, I thought I cherished, turned out to be a fairytale hoax.

How could this be?

Believing love would be all in the air and everywhere, suffocating.
He was the husband, limiting the oxygen.
Life-threatening.

Follow his rules as a wife, 'Do as I say, not as you think.'
He was the husband, the supreme commander.
Unbelievable.

It's not working. He won't listen. I don't matter.
Maybe we can work this out?

Thinking change could be an option, it was not.
He was the husband, the ruler of the house.
Inconceivable.

Expecting understanding was to agree to disagree to a degree, wrong!
He was the husband, 'My way or the highway!'
Help.

I should have known, his actions have shown.
He was the husband, 'Obey or get out of the way.'
Shut up!

I'm fed up.

Patience was lacking on both sides 'cause there
was no understanding.

He was the husband, 'Do as I say, it's only my way.'
Ignorance.

Don't live like this, the husband ruling with an iron fist.
Failure.

The solution?

Communicate, I am the wife, you are the husband, this is a
partnership not a dictatorship.

Dialogue wears well if you listen, and if it's exercised.

If the husband won't listen, perhaps it's time to get
out of the kitchen?

Hell Raiser

*They say opposites attract, that's not always true.
Hell raisers attract hell raisers since I became one,
married to you.*

*The more they nitpick the more I retaliate.
No more false believin', it's time to get even.
Land on my turf, you've got to bite the dirt.*

*There's no truce, just this hell raiser to let loose.
It takes one to know one, not hard to find, it really began
when you messed with my mind.*

*Here we go again with your sarcastic remarks, this is where
the hell raising always starts.*

A Slave Was Made

Blindness for sight.

A man of morals and charisma, was a guiding light yet he became a nightmare overnight.

What made me answer "yes" to his beck and call?

Seemed like right logic for me, he always made it seem right.

He was the head of the house, I obeyed, day and night!

A Slave and Maid Has a Prayer

*You were so negative toward me every day.
Throughout the years, it brought me so many tears.
I fought back and reacted to your disgusting words.*

You were so negative toward me, it leaves me to think it was simply envy.

I learned to laugh more often at what you said, especially before going to bed.

*So many nights I thought I must get out of your evil lair.
It started and ended with a prayer.*

*Lord Jesus Christ,
Thank you for this beautiful day.
Guide my thoughts on what I think and on what I say!
The enemy likes to pierce, kill and steal my joy,
that's his wicked ways.*

*Lord Jesus Christ,
just keep me shielded from harms way, this I do pray.
I am so ready for a new day.
I'll laugh like thunder and my tears like rain
will wash away.*

As though lightning dried them out this day.

My smile will be like the rainbow, and as the day ends, the moon will dim for me to rest and sleep.
You are my shining armor, you are out of sight.
By my side day and night.
When I fall you lift me up, a lesson learned no matter what.
Thank you God, for saving me today.

He Seeks the Weak

The devil is a clever spirit!
He preys on your intelligence.
He introduces you to the opposite of good, making you look back wondering how you stood.

With blinders on he loves to play, creating challenges for you day to day.

He does what he can to undermine the strong.

He mentors the weak, those he artfully seeks.

Only the strong will survive, provided you allow God to revive.

Seek the Good seven days a week, it starts with a simple tweak.

Focus your mind on the One who's above, the one and only, the definition of Love.

I am a Victor

*Surrounded in darkness, captured by evil, he ever thrived,
as I barely survived.*

*I had been victimized by the villain
and became his victim.*

*It's hard to conceive.
He was a villain in the flesh to
deceive and for people to believe.*

*He was greater than himself
for the villain was narcissistic and sadistic.
He was always wearing a disguise and telling lies.*

*Knowing God is my Father has led me to the path
of the light, this place where everything seems
and is so bright.*

*I can see.
I can see enough to get to know me.*

*He called me victorious, that's how I feel and I am secure,
knowing this feeling is actually real.*

I celebrate being victorious, no longer pouting.

Victory is my motto, shouting,
"I am a victor."

Yes, yes, yes, I experience freedom of speech,
I am set free, writing history.

I am a victor.
Steady and focused, am I.
Thanks to my Lord and Savior Jesus Christ He protects me
by and by.

Amen and Amen.

Anxiety

Anxiety has been a struggle inside of me,
tearing me apart.
It's hard to know which way to go,
it's like a maze inside my head.

Where am I to be?
Will I ever get there?
Not if I stay full of anxiety.

Without

I wish I can be kissed.
I wish I can have total bliss.
These are some of the things I miss.

When I think about all of my needs,
I seem to frown and feel down.

Those mid-life years were my prime and
I should not have wasted my time.

The hormones in my body were like a time bomb itching
and kicking, waiting to explode for the man I thought
would love me whole.

Now that I am old, I feel shame to expose all my needs to
the right man if he was willing to please.

So as the days go by, I try and think of why?

Why did I let myself be deprived by this man
I once idolized?

My answer just came to my mind,
I was his concubine.

What's in it for Me?

When you come around it seems you want to stick around.
But when I undress, it seems to digress.
So, what's in it for me?

It carries the length but doesn't make much sense.
But what's in it for me?

You would believe it has a disguise, sometimes it would rise,
but when I arrive it goes back inside.
So, what's in it for me?

I think there's a problem that needs to be fixed.
I feel it's not me, but your old tricky dick.
Be a tiger, get some Viagra.
See if that will do the trick for your old tricky dick.

Come back and see me again,
I'll let you know if there is anything in it for me!

What's Wrong with You?

Taking my vagina for granted, expecting me to spread eagle every time you feel like a hero.
What's the problem with your libido?

What's wrong with you?

Try a little soft peter, and chill to make sex sweeter.
What's wrong with you?

Not romancing me to get ready. Giving me orders when I am nowhere feeling like calling you daddy.
What's wrong with you?

Not respecting yet always expecting.
What's wrong with you?

Your problem is no longer my fear, cause I want you to hear.

No romance without finance, no romance without consideration and there's no hesitation.

Just NO romance without love, no romance without a hug.
No romance, no romance, no romance without these above.

Then figure it out baby…
Our romance is very dull.
To think you had the gall, to think this was a ball,
but baby, not at all.

Do You Mean It?

*What comes out of your mouth has been injected
from within.
Remember, if you must say something,
say what you want to speak into existence.
Don't speak what you do not mean.*

The vision is the incision that you lock into your life.

*Experience is not what happens to a wo/man,
it is what a wo/man does with what happens to her or him.*

*I'm telling you to put on your big girl panties
or your big boy boxers,
and
Use this formula!*

*B-R-A
Believe, Receive, then Achieve.
Believe in yourself.
Receive your gift.
Achieve your goal.*

Every single day, stay on a roll.

Mind

What matters is, mind over matter.

*Dig deep and open up your mind
to the true genius in you.*

*No matter what your field is, rely on and develop the part of
your mind that needs to be balanced.*

There's untold knowledge there in your mind.

*Don't be oppressed or silenced in your mind or
with your mouth.*

Don't waste the matter that matters.

Work it because the mind is a beautiful thing to explore.

Hello, Holler, Holla

*To all people that have and are experiencing
physical, emotional or mental abuse,
Get out!
Get out a-s-a-p!
and
Use this formula!
B-F-F
Believe, Faith, Forgive.
Believe in God and in yourself.
Have faith in God and in yourself.
Forgive them and forgive you.
For without me, where would I be without believing and
having faith?*

Dear Dr. Jiggly Wiggly

*When my mate drinks too much, he starts arguments about
nothing, and every now and then he calls me fat.
When he calls me fat it hurts, causing me to eat more
desserts, then I'm unable to fit in my skirts.
I'm feeling more and more hungry every day and it's time
for him to pay.*

*I hate to feel I can't talk to my mate.
I ate to feel I have to hesitate.
I ate to continue to feel I think it's over.
I ate to continue to feel. I ate.
But it's all over and I ate.
In my dream, I just ate my mate.
Damn, he's gone!
Ain't I full?*

Dr. Wiggly's Response:

*Dear Miss Rounder,
My advice to you is, showing him is better than telling him.
Try playing "**I Got a New Attitude**," by Patti LaBelle.
If that doesn't work, give him a mirror, some Tic Tacs,
a cookbook, a can and a microwave.
Allow plenty of space to pile up the dirty clothes
for him to take to the laundry mat.
Just see how long he will survive before
he cleans up his act.*

I Eat

I sit. I eat.
I exercise my arms from mouth to plate, that
movement is really great.
I walk to the toilet.

I walk to the kitchen, I open the fridge to see what's there.
I walk to my chair so that I eat more.
I sit. I eat.

I watch television, those commercials remind me to get up
from the chair. Where is the meat? It's time for a treat!
I have one three times a day.
I sit. I eat.

Some days, I'll add three more to help hunger
pains go away.
I sit. I eat.

These are the exercises that keeps me growing.
These are the exercises that keeps me going.
These are the exercises that will help me get a death date.
I sit. I eat.

My, my, time does fly.
Bye bye.

Smaller Caboose

I eat because I'm happy,
I eat because I'm sad.

I eat because I do not like myself--
it causes certain parts of my anatomy to grow too fast.

I make excuses to take a seat,
I make excuses to eat.

Excuses don't need to be on repeat,
they cannot be the reason I eat.

My denial had been true indeed,
I will survive going forward and
eat only what I need.

My needs will override my wants and
my wants will decrease as they begin to cease.

Cutting back earns respect, causing less upset.

Eating less allows me to regroup, seeing the whole picture
with a smaller caboose.

Really?

*You complain about how unhappy you are,
yet you stay.*

*It seems to me, it's what you have been wanting
day by day.*

*But you know you are living a lie, a blind person can see it,
so can I.*

*If you keep on complaining
you remain the same, which is a low-down dirty shame.*

Your happiness is your unhappiness.

*Reverse the script.
Come on now and do a triple flip.*

*Love you, it's time for you to!
Love you, it's time for you too!*

When you praise, you raise. It's up to you, boo!

Yes, really!

The Eraser

Take that pencil and paper out.
Write down all your thoughts,
those things done and said, and those what nots.

Write down your sins, even if you feel shame, after all who really is to blame?

Ask God, our Father for forgiveness, to take away the blame and the shame.

Ask God to be your Eraser.

If you believe God has the power to set you free,
it truly will come to be.

Spend some time in praise, as you raise all your concerns to Him.

No more time for feeling mean, it's all clear and clean.
And every day remember,
God is the Eraser.

Secrets Don't Serve

Have you been a secret keeper?
If so, it's an invitation from the grim reaper.
Secrets make it easier to control, they take away your urges to be bold.

At times you may want to pick up the phone and call someone. Other times you may just want to run.
None of these life or death choices are ever fun.

When you need space, you must pick up the pace and go to a safe place.
Wherever you are God is.

Tips for Connection:

Before worship, speak to God.
Ask, share and tell. Then listen.
When you do that all will be well, as He can guide you on who or what else you need to tell.

There are many reasons I stayed, right or wrong, but I'm here to tell you, it just can't go on.

In Matthew 11:28 Jesus said,
"Come to me all of you who are weary and carry a heavy burden and I will give you rest."

I did just that.
It worked for me and it can work for you, too.

Power of the Tongue

*When you think or speak something out loud,
you give life to what you're saying.
That allows it to take root and if you keep saying it,
eventually it becomes your reality.*

Realize it or not, you're prophesying your future.

*Ask God to search your heart for any discouragement and
to take it away, eliminating its destructive powers from you.*

Remember, every new level, there's a new devil.

Stay focused.

Remember, your behind always follows you!

*"Death and life are in the power of the tongue-
they that love it shall eat the fruit thereof."
Proverbs 18:21*

Eyes

Look into my eyes.
Can you see?
Love and affection surrounded by disappointments
and fear that scare me.

I didn't like what I was seeing, didn't like how I was living.
Not good enough, living like that was more than tough.

Love conquers all, so I start to stand tall.

I added more drops of love and affection,
washing out the fear, clinging to the good and positive,
bringing them ever-near.

Love conquers all.

Look into my eyes. What do you see?
Eyes full of love, tears full of joy.
When I open my eyes now I can see,
faith and eyes are working together, harmoniously.

Amazing

*It's amazing how You created life
knowing the knowing before it's a growing.*

*Knowing the ending just like the beginning.
Knowing is the seed inside of me.*

*I wonder what's my future to be, wishing I could see like
You the Almighty!*

*Then I wouldn't trip over the mistakes in life, walking into
those many weeds.
It's a mystery every day of my life.
It is a catastrophe when I ignore the signals
planted inside of me.*

*Great and mighty could I be if it was you ruling me –
then I could walk over eggshells without cracks.
No hurts just perfect peace.
Silence, receiving and listening.*

*I cannot see like You but what I feel is very real.
You tell me to treat each day as the last day and to treasure
each new venture in my life.
You are amazing.*

*Though it all remains a mystery,
I'm learning to trust you, not me.*

Evidently

Are you where you are supposed to be?
Evidently.

Wherever you are, it is where you are supposed to be.
This is one of the best places to be when you are at your worst.
When what you've been doing isn't working,
it's time to change, Evidently.

Want to change your space?
It's time to enter the bigger race.

Start here:

Father, help us to honor Your name.
Come and set up Your kingdom.
Forgive our sins, as we forgive everyone who has done wrong to us and keep us from being tempted.
Give us each day the food, shelter, trust, faith and action we need, and guide us where you would have us grow.

By myself I cannot know, Evidently.

Appreciation

I ask for forgiveness -

*Oh Supportive and Loving Father,
I know You are here for your children and that You love us.
Whether we are right or wrong, You love us.*

*You guide us in the right direction whether we like it or not.
Yes, it is called tough love.
As we face the many challenges in life, You lead us through
the strife when we choose Your path.*

*Please forgive me.
Even when I lie or act like I can't see, you are still loving
me... Thank You for allowing the stop signs, u-turns and
clear directions.
My goal is to follow Thee.*

*Thank You for telling me. Thank You for showing me.
You hear my cry. You lift me up.
Thank You for your presence. Thanks for Your power.
Thanks for Your love.
I am listening.*

You are a great Father.
Even when I lie or act like I can't see,
God You know the true me.
It is a good feeling to be aware of Your presence.
Thank you.

To feel Your support and love when I am right or wrong,
it is a good feeling to be protected by Your presence.
Thank you.

Rainbows

*While looking out the window on this rainy day,
waiting for a rainbow to suddenly display.
The thunder sounded like a roaring lion next door.
The lightning was sharp and electrifying
as though someone snapped my picture and
they thought it was okay.*

*The raindrops kept falling to the rhythm of a
reggae steel drum, eyes open and listening in awe.
It's an amazing setting, the ozone is zero,
the raindrops are so crystal clear.
Only God's super powers we see without fear.*

*This is a blessing to live in this place,
how sweet the sound,
God's voice whispering in our ear.
It's so amazing to let love spread like the air.
Wrapped by faith and grace, it's soothing.
Salvation is everywhere.*

*Don't you think this is amazing?
That's how God wanted it to be
serving our Father, the Almighty Majesty.
Now that's amazing to me.
Then suddenly it appeared, the rainbow.*

Know No

Know when to say no.

Yes, it's two little letters, sure to ruffle some feathers.

No is a strong word that needs to be heard.
No is a big little word.

Saying no with meaning brings respect.
The respondee may say, "What the heck?"

Go on and say it, "No!"
Using this word is not for show.

Just say "No, no, no, no and no!"
You might even add, "It's time for you to go!"

Say it. Own it. Work it. Clone it!

No, no and no!
Don't it feel good to know you said no?

Laughing

Laughter is healthy, even if you fake it at first.
Try it, if only in short bursts.

Just start laughing.
Soon it becomes infectious especially when you have company around.

Just start laughing.
It won't be long before everybody is happy, laughing.

Ha, ha, ha, ho, ho, ho, hee, hee, hee.
Go on ahead, laugh,
I know you want to laugh with me.

The Key

*The key to a successful marriage is to
see no evil, hear no evil
and
do no evil.*

*The key to get out of this marriage successfully is to see all
evil, hear all evil
speak all evil
and
do all evil.*

*You will need to get out of this
ASAP!*

Getting to the New Me

*I've grown sick and tired of the old me.
It's time to change and be a new me!*

Too many times I would cry, feeling as if I was just going to die, I held on questioning the source of my destiny.

I want out of this old life. It's been filled with too much strife.

It captured my self-esteem. Now it's time to wake up and know it's not a dream.

No longer do I want to be controlled, as I often wonder how it feels to be bold.

Ouch, that hurt. That enemy is fierce. It's not okay for him to pierce.

I want to be sifted by GOD, as I learn to be and to love me.

I know my heart is fair. I know my brain is there, though so many times I wondered where!

With the new me, I grow and learn to help others be!

I look at some people and they look sad.
I want them to know not everything is bad.

Getting to the new me makes me and others glad. Even when stuff happens it's not all bad.

I compliment them to change their persona for a while.
Sometimes they respond saying, I made their day or with a smile.
I want to help any way I can, as we all need a helping hand.

Getting to the new me has always been part of my destiny.
It was just difficult to see.

Moving Along

It's me, myself and I that's holding me back.
Can't let go of the past.
It's still just kicking my ass.
Want to remedy this quick, but it just sticks.

Getting to the root will open my door.
Let's finish the ending by dealing with why the seed was a horrific beginning.

Those seeds planted when you were young, sometimes just need to be over and done.

Leave it alone, you can make it.
Have faith in the Man upstairs and in yourself.
Start thinking, let you mind be new technology, not based on old geography.

Move it along, let's rejoice and sing happy songs,
"Oh happy day, when Jesus washed all my sins away."

Divorce

*Now that I'm divorced, single and free, I don't have the
abstractions subtracting from me.*

*Living each day as my last, enjoying it all and remembering
only the good from my past.
I wish him well for his new beginning, after all, we are over.
The end is here.*

*I say to myself, take some advice.
Go travel, get a makeover, eat healthy, exercise and
ride a bike.*

*Do things that truly are positive for you. Even try and be a
little selfish too. It won't hurt.*

*Believe me let gratitude always be your attitude each
day of your life.*

*'Cause God is your Father, He always gives good advice.
So life goes on, I'm living single and free,
I'm praying for my new beginning.
I am praying for my new me!*

#MeToo

Oprah Winfrey inspired me to write this poem on the day she spoke at the 75th Annual Golden Globe Awards. Though it happened when I was 72 years old, I felt like the little girl in me got a new level of courage and bravery. I cried tears of joy and relief, lifting my belief.

#MeToo

I am with me.
Are you too?
Doesn't seem that way, Boo Boo.

#MeToo has shown me that it's about me believing in me and in speaking on #MeToo.

What a wonderful feeling to say:
Me, myself and I spoke up loud, proud and clear:

Stop It.
I ain't.
I can't.
I won't.
But I will expose you, Boo Boo.
#MeToo

Grudges

Gossiping allows words that are blown out of proportion,
often causing misunderstanding.

Grudges develop through hurts, adding so many fats.

Carrying a grudge adds on pounds.

Exercising with prayer takes them away.

Every one of us is guilty in some form or fashion.

Forgiveness feathers your weight.
Take those and give them to God.

Go to the source and talk, without anger,
starting a well-balanced diet.

One thing you must learn is to have faith and love God,
love yourself and have love for one another,
then accountability starts.

Being lighter makes every single day much brighter.

A Recipe for Grace

The dos and don'ts!

*Get your own recipe,
Do what it takes to be the best lady or man you can be.*

*Add your own ingredients like
love, respect, honesty and dignity.
Then blend well.
Next, sprinkle on conversations with Christ,
something we all don't touch on much.*

This recipe makes great vittles for all.

It spices up your life and it's a delight!

Birth of a Child

Up to now I had been enslaved.
I was in bondage in my mother's womb enslaved as a child
– she carried me for nine months.

Molested, vulnerable to deception.
That's what happened to me when I was five.

Lord Jesus Christ didn't want us to be born or live this way.

It was a set up for failure.

Just call me a procrastinator, never no more.
It was the devil for sure. My God opens doors.

My eyes are no longer shut. My ears hear the message. My heart beats strong. My mind believes. My soul dances.
My Spirit prances.

Don't worry about anything but pray for everything. This is my guide and you will surely survive.
Thank you Lord Jesus Christ.
I feel wonderfully alive.

If you have been molested and you've been through a lifetime of pain and deception, just know God doesn't want you to live like that. Staying in it is not what He wants. He wants you to survive. Keep praying to him, do what you are supposed to do – don't just talk.

I had little faith, yet I am still here.

It took a lifetime for me to be reborn.

Why Did I Stay?

*"People have asked, "Why did I stay?
My answer? I don't know."*

When I started thinking hard about why I stayed, I came up with a few answers, not excuses, answers. His words were more damaging than the physical abuse, although the pain was difficult to tolerate. Because of the "daily programming" of his harmful words that made it easier for him to physically injure me, and for me to stay, too afraid to go. The treatment changed my whole character.

18 Ways Manipulation Kept Me Bound

1. A Slave – I allowed him to treat me like a slave. I waited on him hand and foot. He would say, "Go get it (his food!)" or "Go fix it (his plate)" and "Go do it (vacuuming so much the hose seemed to be attached to my butt)."
2. Helpless – I didn't know what, when or how to stop the fear in my head. I felt numb.
3. Self-Doubt – I felt I didn't have the courage to leave.
4. Bad Choices – My poor choices in men were thinking "He has a good job. I can change him into not being as strict of a husband."
5. Sanity Questioned - He always accused me of living in fairy tale land, making me question myself and begin to believe his lies.

6. Ugly – He told me I didn't know how to dress; and if my hair was not fixed like he wanted it I would have to go back to the hairdresser to get a different style, and sometimes a different beautician.
7. Unwanted – He told me no one would want me.
8. Sad – He said I couldn't make it without him and called himself the *Rock of Gibraltar*.
9. Isolation – I would always ask if it's okay to go with my friends and he would tell me, "Those bitches don't have husbands and they want you to not have one. They are single and they mean you no good." My friends would tell me, "He ain't your daddy. You are a grown ass woman."
10. Belief – I lost belief in myself and started believing him. He said he was the husband and the husband was to lead. He taught me to follow, that resulted in me becoming hollow.
11. Alone – I felt alone even when he was at home. He would look or stare at me as if he hated me. Especially when he was inebriated, he would still insist he was "right" though both of us knew what he was saying and doing was very wrong.
12. Money – When he criticized me, I would begin to find other outlets to release the anxiety. Twisting parts of my body with his hands or bruising me and then saying later he was sorry and wouldn't do it again was too much for me to take. It was all lies. But the money he gave me to make up for the abuse provided freedom until the next time.

A FORGIVING HEART MOVES FORWARD

13. Double Standards – He would tell me he could do no wrong and he would get respect because he was "Mr." but if I did wrong, I would always be a nobody.
14. Faking It – He told me not to show hurt or pain on my face. He said I needed to do that because no one would know if he was in pain, because he always smiled.
15. Belittling – He said all my poetry is generic. I wanted more support from him. Every day, his words and actions were tearing me down, instead of building me or my children up.
16. Brainwashing – He would tell me and my children that we wouldn't even have food to eat, if it were not for him. He controlled every aspect of our lives, even though I maintained a job too.
17. Inferiority Complex – I didn't know me anymore. I became bitter and always felt as if I was not good enough.
18. Abusiveness – I was used to the abusiveness. It was part of the marriage even on vacations. His favorite words were, "Get over it."

If you suspect someone is in an abusive situation, it will be difficult for you to understand why they stay, even frustrating. Remember, the "programming" doesn't happen overnight. I'm sharing some of my experiences so that you can consider what your loved one or yourself might be up against. You must combat it. Get help. Tangible help.

"If you find yourself or someone you know experiencing these signs of abuse, behaviors or thoughts, don't do what I did for 50 years. Don't stay, go!"

Reality Check

"The journey through abuse is extremely difficult but you can make it to the other side. First, consider what's going on in your mind, and take time to decide in courage rather than in fear."

1. Bullying – I felt horrible when he would say insulting things in front of people and then turn around and say, "Can't you take a joke?"
2. Emotionally – I felt alone, nowhere to go. Walls were closing in.
3. Spiritually – Deep down inside of me, I knew God loved me and wanted me to hear His voice. He showed me repeatedly but I was blind and couldn't see nor hear.
4. Damage – I was damaged goods with no self-worth camouflaging the real me.
5. Insecure – I felt I couldn't make it without him. I was nothing, just a rag doll.
6. Confused – I didn't know if I was right or wrong, if I was coming or going.
7. Shameful – I felt ashamed of myself and that I was an embarrassment for him.
8. Catharsis – Finally releasing and getting rid of my strong repressed emotions and it feels good. Releasing and letting go is a daily process.

When someone does and says hurtful things to you, they are describing what's deep inside of them and hating on themselves, directing it at you.

Pray

Pray for them and pray for peace to be still in you, so that you can figure out what to do. Also remember, *God is the Eraser* so ask Him to help you forgive yourself, giving you strength and courage to overcome lingering mind tricks.

Scripture to carry you through:

> *"Let not an evil speaker be established in the earth,*
> *evil shall hunt the violent man to overthrow him."*
> Psalm 140:11

> *"By this I know that You are pleased with me,*
> *because my enemy does not shout in triumph over me."*
> Psalm 41:11

Affirmation for the aftermath:

I am no longer a slave without a brain.
I fled from what was holding me back.
Better now than never.
My body, mind and soul started undergoing a
transformation becoming a human, being.
Emerging into a strong, gifted woman
I am treasuring and loving me.
Better now than never.
I am better now than ever.

About the Author

Shelia Mansfield was born in St. Louis, Missouri, and spent a few years in sunny Southern California being a mother and working in the aeronautics industry before returning to her hometown, where she's lived for most of her life. Being molested as a young girl affected the way she saw herself and men. Married early and divorced late, in between she lived a holy-hell of a life. Now in her 70s, hers is a story of surviving two abusive marriages, consuming nearly 50 years. She was encouraged to write poetry as a means to stay alive, express herself and to increase her self-esteem. Shelia's favorite symbol is the elephant, the strong yet ever gentle and wise spirit animal, which exemplifies focused power and strength, which inspired the book cover.

A Forgiving Heart Moves Forward is an insightful poetic journey designed to acknowledge struggles and offer inspiration and courage to any person who has been in abusive relationships. The author says, *"Burned by a fire? Who lit the flame? Someone is to blame. Is it a shame or do you walk away sane?"* and if they are hell-bent, *"Ditch it if it ain't worth fixin."*

Notes

Notes

Notes

Notes

Notes

www.ingramcontent.com/pod-product-compliance
Lightning Source LLC
Chambersburg PA
CBHW050443010526
44118CB00013B/1663